Lenses

Seeing the Unseen Spaces Between Us

JEREMY WRIGHT

In Memory Of

Terrance J. Irons
Mary Alice Wright
Caleb M. Blake
Rev. Sonja C. Irons, M. Div.

Lenses:

Seeing the Unseen Spaces Between Us

©2021 Jeremy Wright

print ISBN: 978-1-66781-994-5
ebook ISBN: 978-1-66781-995-2

Book Intention and The Seed of You

The intention of this book is to help you "SEE" the positive intent and deeper meaning of the circumstances and people in your life. Trust the process and its unfolding; the positive intent and deeper meaning of circumstances and people are hidden lessons readying you for your purpose in life. Losing a friendship, a rejection letter on the 15th job application, the 99th no when pitching your business idea, the horrible employment experience, the absence of a parent, the untimely death of a family member or friend, the break up of a relationship, the ruined credit score, and more are circumstances with positive intent and a hidden lesson. That coworker that immediately becomes a family member, that friend that intentionally stays in the same cycle of poor choices, the boss that makes you question if the benefits and rewards of your job are worth it, the person who cuts you off in traffic, the person who asks what you do for a living when you do not look like their typical clientele, the person who you randomly meet and become instant lifelong friends with, the stranger who gives you exactly what you need at that moment, your family, and more all have a positive intent and a hidden lesson. I have grown to learn that life is a two-way street as everyone ends up in a circumstance, causing them to cross paths for a reason; remember, you are not the only person with a life and a purpose.

Circumstances and people are helping you, although we may not be able to see this on the surface. Sometimes it's apparent, and sometimes it is not. Still, I assure you, if you pause before you react, you can shift your lens to "SEE" the unseen spaces between you, your circumstances, and the people in your life. The ability to pause before you react comes from The Secret Garden that I described in *A Gift of Peace and Purpose: A Survivor's Journey and Love and Meditation: The Keys to Manifestation*. To clarify, there is the physical see, for those of us blessed with the sense of sight, and there is the spiritual "SEE" that takes a holistic view of life from a place of self-awareness to recognize the positive intent and understand the deeper meaning of what is in front of you. Your lens is formed through how your life has unfolded up until this present moment which includes every circumstance and every person. Everything knowingly or unknowingly shapes the lens that you look out of.

Without self-awareness or allowing our higher sense of self to lead, we go through life looking through a physical lens of survival to see what is in front of us to keep ourselves alive. Allowing your higher sense of self to lead allows you to look through a spiritual lens of self-awareness to "SEE" the positive intent and deeper meaning behind each circumstance and people in your life; The Secret Garden is crucial to this. It takes patience and practice to shift from seeing through your physical lens to your spiritual lens. Without loving yourself enough to clear the physical, mental, and spiritual space in your life, it becomes challenging to shift from one lens to the other. Sometimes your lens can become fractured through trauma. This trauma, in hindsight, presents the opportunity to peel back layers of who you thought you were to get to the core of who you indeed are.

In *A Gift of Peace and Purpose*, I label this process as "The Seed of You," upon which this book rests. This process allows one to dig deep into their circumstances and the people in their lives so that lessons can be identified, learned, and applied in pursuit of one's life purpose. Like any seed, you must go through your process to be whatever you will be without concern about how and when. This process requires consistent reflection and meditation on the unseen spaces between circumstances, people, and you as they all point to your purpose. Although it may feel uneasy when releasing control of the how and when, trusting the process and its unfolding is necessary to allow the lessons you will learn from circumstances and people to pull towards and ready you for your purpose. At the end of this brief, light-hearted yet highly impactful continuation from *A Gift of Peace and Purpose: A Survivor's Journey*, you will "SEE" the Unseen Spaces Between Us, and you may be positive that your life will never be the same.

Dear Me,

We are elevating higher and higher each round. It seems the higher we elevate spiritually, the more everything becomes magnified. The more we cleanse ourselves of things that clutter our life or pull us away from our purpose, the more intense our purpose, gifts, and talents become. Of course, with everything, there must be balance; the existence of equally extreme opposites. This is apparent when we experience these "swings" of low points as life unfolds.

We must give ourself grace knowing that we are a spiritual beings having a human experience. Thus, we are subject to stumbling sometimes. Having the self-awareness to view what we are going through holistically, as we stumble, is a gift many may never experience. I am proud of us for taking baby step after baby step to get to where we are, even if it took a while to get there. The important thing is that we make it to our destination, purpose fulfilled. But what happens when we "make it" and that which we have affirmed in private manifests? Have we done our due diligence in communicating and setting boundaries? Have we genuinely gotten to the root of all our issues? I feel the honest answer is no because this is an ongoing process.

When will the "right time" ever happen? The simple answer is, there is no right time; it simply happens when it happens. Just keep taking baby steps, it's not easy, but I feel that it will be well worth it to the core. Looking at the attitude of society pertaining to mental health, there seems to be a shift for the better. Celebrities are sharing their stories of childhood trauma, hurt, pain, and more making it "okay" to talk about these issues.

Hearing people like Taraji P. Henson, Will Smith, and Adele coming forth and sharing their stories, Beyoncé making anthems about truly being alive despite all that you've been through, Issa Rae depicting real life in film, Oprah and Prince Harry making documentaries to share what people go through, and platforms such as *The Real*, *The Breakfast Club*, and *Red Table Talks* talking about mental health is needed; it is a collective effort for a greater good. The tides are shifting positively for those who have been suffering in the dark; this is the confirmation we need to keep pressing forward; we can help too. Even when it doesn't feel like we are equipped to handle what may come, everything will be alright. Through the course of nature and all that is the divine source, everything we need comes from within. The light at the end of the tunnel seems like it's been so close for so long. The difference is, when I close my eyes to visualize what I desire, I feel the warmth of the sun. We are almost there.

With all the unconditional love from within,
The ME behind me

Dear Reader,

Hold on. I know life has not been easy. I hope that this book will help you better navigate the path you are on to get through life a little easier. I am writing this book to help you disrupt the pattern of living in survival mode by offering my life as a reference point. Grinding everyday to survive makes it almost impossible to take time to truly process what is going on in our lives. Knowing that we are in control of our destinies, we owe it to ourselves to dig deep for life's lessons.

This is not an easy journey, but one well worth it. We all need tools, ideas, theories, or whatever works for us to get through this thing called life. Pointing out things that we all experience in life, I hope you can walk away changed for the better. You reading this book is a sign that positive change is possible and closer than you think. Hang in there. I'll walk by your side.

With all of the unconditional love that I have,

Jeremy

Author Updates

Before I get into what is going on with me, how are you? How is life? Are you slowing down and allowing your higher sense of self to lead? Have you decided to walk down The Golden Path? Are you practicing your definition of love, meditation, and manifestation? How has your life changed? Are you practicing self-care? I know it is not easy, but I assure you, a wall can only withstand so many hits before it falls, keep swinging. I am slowly but surely knocking down my personal walls that have been put up over years and years of trauma and not addressing things as they should've been addressed. This is ongoing, and no one should feel bad about doing what is best for them. My uncle, Charles Wright, Jr., is an excellent example of this. He's a cancer survivor, a veteran, and has struggled with a lot of hurt, pain, and addiction, and I imagine his life has taken many twists and turns trying to piece things together again.

In our conversations, he shares with me his desire to do the right thing, but because of past trauma, it is difficult; keep swinging, Uncle Charles. In my previous book, I visualized having my family under one roof as we spend time together, create business ideas, pass down traditions, and build a legacy. I didn't think that would happen so quickly; be careful what you ask for because you just might get it. Thankful for the ability to work from home, my uncle, my mom, Mason, and I were all under one roof in South Carolina. Although it was a bit much for me, given that I am usually by myself, I immediately saw what I spoke only a few months ago come into existence; trust the process and its unfolding. This newfound sense of unity amongst us was an easily recognizable feeling. It matched what I invoked during meditation as I manifested what future family gatherings would feel like.

What was critically important to sustaining the legacy being built was the necessary work we all had to do together. Each person was dealing with their own individual trauma, and collectively, we had family trauma. This required acknowledging and admitting some things that were not easy to do, but it was necessary. Breaking the foundation of what was laid for them made it easy to create a new reality based on truth and not deceit. The common theme amongst us all was hurt people hurting people from generation to generation. Still, now, we can do things differently and better than ever.

There was no need for numbing coping mechanisms because we had each other. There was no need to fulfill an endless void because we were there to do our best to fulfill each other after taking care of our individual needs. This is definitely not an overnight process. Acknowledging, addressing, processing, and releasing trauma was necessary to ensure we laid a foundation that all generations behind us could stand without wavering. Speaking of wavering, so much more has happened since we last spoke, neither good nor bad but simply stuff that happened.

Before I get too deep into what has happened, as stated earlier, the more spiritually aligned I become, the more sensitive I am to environments and people. I pick up on everything even more than I already did. It's almost as if what was in my life physically, spiritually, and emotionally indeed blocked and numbed my ability to operate at a higher sense of self. The more I released to receive, the more in tune I became with myself and thus source. This involved releasing worldly things such as clothes and cars, people, including family and friends, and anything that no longer served me a purpose in pursuit of my purpose in life.

To determine if something no longer served me a purpose, I compared how I felt in the circumstance to the feeling of what I invoked during manifestation and the peace of my secret garden. This barrier kept me in check for the most part, but I am human, as I have said before. Of course, as life would have it, the closer we get to what we desire, life allows circumstances and people to test us on a deeper level and continuously help us learn to ensure we are prepared for it; this never feels good but is very necessary. Sometimes people you would never expect, such as close family and friends, are a part of the process, a true test of the heart. The key to not allowing this to keep you off track is allowing your highest sense of self to lead; trust the process and its unfolding.

Never did I think I would get some of the calls and text messages that I did, never thought I would be called a liar twice, never thought people would respond the way that they did to some of the successes I shared with them, never thought I would be forced to make some of the decisions that I did. Still, I know just as sure as I am typing this book that it all serves a positive intent and deeper meaning that is readying me for my purpose and everything that comes with fulfilling it. Even though I had moments of not being consistent with my routine of ensuring that I take care of myself and manifesting the life that I desire, I still felt the impact of what I had been doing consistently from prior months. I knew this because of moments when particular previous life experiences flashed before my eyes. On the surface, they were the most random things that I could have remembered, but somehow they all tied to my purpose; trust the process and its unfolding. The example that I feel is most relevant was my eighth grade science teacher, Mrs. Sauer, who taught me to protect what was near to my heart while learning something new.

What I took away from this was the ability to be open to things aside from what was taught or very personal. It doesn't mean that you must accept it but listening and exposing yourself to things that allow you to test or validate what you believe makes you stronger. Not having the ability to test or validate what you believe in leaves room to consider a gap somewhere. This random memory from over 20 years ago was a sign that, as humans, our paths may not be written in stone, but our destination was always planned. Our choices on our path determine if we will reach our destiny. What was near and dear to me was a constrained view of what God was through religion.

At such a young age, life did not offer circumstances and people to teach me lessons about God. I was told what God was. Eventually, these lessons would show up as an adult to help me explore things outside of what I was taught and was near my heart. Testing what I was taught God was through my personal experiences has allowed me to embrace that my human mind cannot fathom God in its totality, and thus God is. In reverence of God, I go back and forth with saying source; I'll go into further detail later on. This is a very intense inner battle that I am fighting even at this moment.

When I hear people say "God will take care of it" or "God can do all things," I feel conflicted because that suggests that God is comprehensible and focused on our individual circumstances. I genuinely feel that separating ourselves and putting the work on God leaves room for us to sit back and not act. This constant separation of self and God also makes it easier for us to "blame God" when things go wrong. When things do not go according to our plans, our spiritual lens allow us to "SEE" that it is us not in alignment with God, the divine source that fuels endless possibility. When there is a misalignment, we are simply fueling possibility on a limited source: ourselves. We fuel ourselves with things that are not in alignment with our purpose such as materialistic things, titles, surface relationships, facades and more. Thus, we end up in circumstances and with people that have to break us and put us back in alignment with that which is incomprehensible: God. Without God, the electricity in our lives means we must operate on our own batteries, which eventually die because of no charge. To me this is where poor mental health, diseases, and other body related issues can happen forcing us to slow down and reevaluate our actions.

On a lighter note, my mom got a toy poodle named Mason. Mason has been here before, and in fact, I told my mom, "You don't realize what you did when you named Mason." I still stand by that statement. Mason's name came from combining the name of my grandmother Mary Alice and my aunt Sonja. As I stated, Mason has been here before.

I believe everything that we name and define truly has meaning as what we speak has power that comes from God. I've never been more scared to name my kids. Mason has taught me so much, more so patience, being present, and going after what you want. Have you ever walked a dog in a new area that they have not smelled? Mason smells as far as Venus, and it takes forever for him to take care of business. This has required me to practice patience, helping me stop to breathe deeply and be present.

Now, instead of getting frustrated, I take the time to manifest walking in my future neighborhood. I close my eyes and try to visualize what the houses look like, what it feels like to have genuinely lovely, caring, and respectful neighbors, a beautiful lake, and a well-kept gated community. I think I'll go with Toll Brothers—I love watching walk-throughs of their houses on Youtube. I especially like watching Enes Yilmazer and the team tour beautiful mansions and yachts around the world. It is because they do such a great job I use their videos as a means to help visualize what my reality will look like. Knowing that acquiring this would take work, my four-legged little brother comes through with another lesson.

Whenever Mason hears the words "treat" or "walk" or smells food, he is laser-focused. He doesn't miss a beat regardless of how long it takes to get what he desires. He will get what he wants. Mason is very consistent with doing what he is taught will yield a particular result. Why is this so hard for us as human beings to follow? Free will and being sourced by a divine higher power—God—is something that we truly have to align and hone in on. I have to admit, juggling so many personal projects, I have lost focus here and there; I am still very human.

Being out of my environment in South Carolina with my mom, uncle, and Mason is teaching me the importance of preparation before work. Since I am a creature of habit, when I left my apartment to stay with my mom for a while, it seemed everything went out of whack. This showed me how easy it is to fall into old habits. My eating habits was terrible, I was not consistently meditating, I wasn't sleeping well, I felt very anxious, my environment challenged me to be even more disciplined. Yet another lesson amongst all of this, teach and demonstrate through real-life experience.

Suppose I want to help people operate at their highest potential through self-awareness. How can I do so from a vacuum in my apartment where I controlled everything that happened with a specific rhythm? People need help and me going back into an environment that was challenging for me was a necessary lesson in preparation for what is about to come. I feel coming back home allowed me to start getting things in order. When harvest season comes, my family will not hinder me but help and motivate me to fulfill my purpose so I can obtain what I desire. To get what I desire, I must align my efforts with my purpose in life and not lose focus, regardless of the how or when.

In every circumstance I find myself in, whether it involves people or not, I must actively choose to operate at my highest sense of self by switching to my spiritual lens. I must identify, learn, and apply lessons to take a step closer to fulfilling my purpose in life. I must ensure that I have the capacity to operate and pour into others as I honor my purpose in life. To reap the harvest of one thousand generations, one must sow ten thousand seeds. This is why I want to help you "SEE" the unseen spaces between us.

Release to Receive

Earlier, I alluded to releasing to receive; this has been an ongoing theme for me over the past few years. I have released a lot of worldly stuff. Still, more recently, within the past seven months of writing this, I have been releasing circumstances and people. I realize that in my human expression, during this human experience, I will meet with others in their human expression. To me, the human expression is simply the physical or tangible part of who we interact with daily. The spiritual expression is inward and the human expression is outward.

During our life, we may encounter people, outside of our family, who we click with. These types of relationships make it easier for us to get through life. Sometimes I feel we get too caught up in ensuring that our human expressions are intertwined and comfortable with one another. We forget that we are spiritual beings with a purpose limited by the life of our human expression. This realization has helped me release family and friends that no longer serve a purpose in helping me obtain my purpose in life. I don't take it personally and hope they don't either. Still, boundaries must be created, even with people who are very close to us.

Looking at these relationships and demonstrating love in action has helped me realize some personal triggers that I didn't realize were there. In *Love and Meditation*, I spoke about triggers being an opportunity to reflect inward to understand the root of what caused you to react a certain way. We have to make it a habit of working on the root of our triggers because not doing so will make it easier to lose everything you obtain. It's never easy but worth the long-term gain; trust the process and its unfolding. Being able to recognize my triggers and retreat into my secret garden allows me to react more appropriately. That space between what has happened "to me" and my reaction makes it easier to also detach.

Over these past seven months of 2021, I have really been trying to understand the why behind things and detaching as I need to. When I say detach, I mean releasing a death grip on things so that there is room for growth and expansion. I would consider it the same as shedding unnecessary weight as I have been doing over the past few years. The most critical thing is understanding the why or more profound meaning to why you are attached to it, to begin with. The most essential thing that I have learned to detach from are the words. Simple words like time which I'll go into later.

These ongoing themes in my life, such as trusting the process and its unfolding, releasing to receive, and detaching, almost make it seem like I am being wrapped up in a cocoon. Almost like life is preparing me for something that requires me to not have such a firm grasp on little things. I thought that I had already gone through a stage of metamorphosis, but it seems as though my life requires me to go deeper. To me, a metamorphosis of self is a deep retreat within oneself to come out better. It's not isolating yourself from others but genuinely taking time to reflect on life, decisions, and more in a profound way.

It would make sense that I had to shed, release, and detach as I enter a phase of my life that requires giving attention to myself. I don't know what this looks like, but I am readying myself for it as best as possible by releasing control of the how and when. To use an analogy, if I center myself, I feel that this metamorphosis of self is necessary because I have become a very self-aware caterpillar dreading going to the next level based on what I have experienced just from waking up, in a sense. Like with the caterpillar in *Alice in Wonderland*, there seems to be an irreversible process started by my own awakening. On the other side of this process is my ability to operate at the next level closer to my true potential; trust the process and its unfolding.

Book of Life

Abstract:

One of many things that we have in common is that we all have life. This alone should create the desire to stick together to make life easier for everyone. Unfortunately, this view isn't held by everyone, and that's okay. We are only responsible for our individual lives and the lives of our children. For those who are open to the idea that life can be easier if we work together, I hope to help you see the unseen spaces between us. We all go through life, starting with what was given to us, which evolves into what happens to us. Within these experiences, we interact with one another, not knowing or trying to understand the deeper meaning of why because we are simply trying to survive. Your purpose pulls you through life by sifting you through circumstances and people to make you ready for it. It's up to you to embrace all parts of your life experience that make the whole of who you are. Just as a seed, you must go through all the necessary phases involving circumstances and people to be what you were always meant to be. Before we get into the central focus of this book, let's take a moment to lay a foundation by looking at some of the things that were given to us and what has happened to us. Answer these questions and reflect:

- What do you think the meaning of life is?

- Are you working towards what you have defined as the meaning of life?

- What is your belief system, and what does it suggest about the meaning of life?

- If your belief system was never taught to you, would you still believe in it?

- Whose belief system is wrong?

- Where do we go after we die?

- What do you gain from this human experience?

- What do you gain from going to work besides money?

- Why do we not teach life skills in school?

- Why are those responsible for educating us in our youth, keeping us alive, and enforcing laws not paid as those who create laws?

- Who benefits from paying years of medical and car insurance when we never get into accidents or have minimal medical issues?

- Who is responsible for ensuring the poor are taken care of?

- Suppose you never made a conscious decision about a topic (it was what it was without question). Is it appropriate to say that someone else made a conscious decision about the same topic when it contradicts what you feel is normal?

- Do things still have the same meaning after we defined what it was within our comprehension?

There are no right or wrong answers to those questions. The intent of those questions is to open your mind to thinking and to reflect. Just as my eighth grade science teacher taught me, protect what is personal to you while still being open to something new.

Chapter of Life as a Process

Quote:

"No matter how or when you bring water to a boil, one must have and use all things necessary to make it happen; trust the process."

Analogy:

Have you seen a lion in person without a cage? I imagine that it is nothing to shrug at as your life can change in seconds. Everyone is obsessed with the lion as the king of the jungle but rarely stops to think about the process it takes. From a cub to an adult, the lion cannot take shortcuts; doing so can be the difference between life and death.

As I continue to learn myself, I recognize that I am a very process-oriented person. In other words, I am the type of person that walks on the sidewalk even when there is a shortcut through the grass; to me, the sidewalk clearly has a purpose. This doesn't mean I am inflexible, but I like structure and space to let things unfold. Until I understand the process, things may not make sense. There is this lingering question of "Why?" until I have a feeling of ease through deep meditation. In my reflection or meditation, I kept asking myself, how does this thing called life work? In my second book *Love and Meditation: The Keys to Manifestation*, I discuss seeing this big picture of life. Looking through a spiritual lens, I believe I have an idea of how things work together so divinely that we can comprehend what I would consider the process of life. I will give you my definition of everything necessary for this process, but I encourage you to define and reshape this process on your own; after all, it is your experience with life and not mine.

Source:

To me, source is the collective of everything. It is you, it is me, it is the animals, it is the trees, it is grass, it is water, it is the clouds, it is the asteroid, it is the stars, it is. Source is not he, source is not she, source is not angry, source is not happy, source is. Suppose source could be anything, according to the laws that hold together our human experience. In that case, there has to be a balance of what you recognize source as. The presence of two halves makes a whole, and thus source is. Source is everything beyond what you define source as, meaning it is incomprehensible, so I simply say source is. We are responsible for labeling and defining things in a way that makes us feel comfortable so that we can comprehend and determine if it is a threat to our lives. This doesn't mean let everything just fall apart but take a step back, breathe, and be okay with things not fitting within our ability to comprehend and fix. Rest comfortably in the fact that source will provide a never-ending flow of limitless possibilities as long as we do the work.

Highest Sense of Self:

To me, the highest sense of self is an internal spiritual expression of source. It is our never-ending connection to source, making us spiritually limitless. We, unlike source, are physically limited in this human experience. Given that we are source and possess a fraction of source, we can navigate life easily if and only if we make room for our highest sense of self to step forward and guide our actions. This limitless spiritual expression connects us all and gives us abilities beyond the comprehension of the human expression. We limit ourselves based on our ability to comprehend through the physical lens. We can shift to our spiritual lens to see limitless possibilities and the unseen spaces between us.

Purpose:

To me, purpose is the personal reason(s) you are here to be of service to the collective human experience. To ensure it is obvious, I'll restate that purpose is not self-serving but an opportunity to serve others. It takes work to identify your purpose. This is especially true when you are not aware of any lens other than your physical lens to see out of. You will know when you have landed on your purpose based on the way it feels and what happens when you are of service to people with that purpose with good intentions. As I stated in

Love and Meditation: The Keys to Manifestation, "Chase your purpose and everything will follow. Chase everything and life will bring you sorrow."

Time and Chance:

To me, I would define time as a continuous spectrum of events that consist of circumstances and people. As things unfold, there is a precise moment when circumstances and people align just right, creating chance. I am growing to accept that time as we have defined it in everyday life is a false reality. We have defined time to help us be productive, but it doesn't have to be that way; we choose for it to be that way. Think of life beyond you. Think of the duck in a pond, think of the shooting star in the sky, and think of the trees as they go through seasons. These things do not adhere to what we have defined as time; they simply unfold without worrying about the how or when. I don't know about you, but it is very rare that I see a duck, star, or tree in distress unless an outside force brings that stress onto it. Just as source simply is, everything outside of our life simply is without adhering to what we define as time; they seem to be just fine. The difference between us and these things is our connection to source, our highest sense of self. Our appropriate and intentional use of our higher sense of self makes life easier. Circumstances that involve people create chance and thus opportunities necessary for us to be readied for our purpose. We often overlook these unseen spaces between us and end up in a cycle of unlearned lessons.

Circumstances and People:

To me, circumstances are a brief snapshot of our life with context. We choose to make circumstances good, bad, or ugly. Circumstances are none of these things; it simply is. People are literally all seven billion of us on this rock we call earth. As stated before, circumstances and people have underlying lessons tied to them that hopefully you learn early on in life rather than later. We cannot learn everything, and that is okay. We can simply do our best to identify, learn, and apply life lessons to be our best selves and be readied for our purpose.

Life Lesson:

To me, a life lesson is a piece of knowledge hidden within circumstances and people that is necessary to equip you to handle your purpose. Without this knowledge, you will not handle your purpose well. Purpose is exceptionally dense and impactful, you must equip yourself to handle it. It's almost like each life lesson you learn gives you a key ingredient to the recipe that illuminates your purpose. There are many life lessons, and I am inclined to say that we will always learn and grow on our spectrum of unfolding events. It wouldn't be life if these life lessons were right before us to quickly identify and learn. The hidden nature of life lessons makes it possible for cycles to be created.

Cycle:

To me, a cycle is an unlearned lesson, within a circumstance, potentially passed down from one generation to the next. It's very plain and straight-forward: what my grandparents learned or did not learn is passed down to my parents through their actions. What my parents did or did not learn is then passed to me through their actions. It is up to me to choose to do things differently, hopefully from a place of self-awareness. When you shift from the physical lens to a spiritual lens, you can clearly see what needs to be done to break cycles. It just becomes a question of if you have the drive to do it. Sometimes cycles are created through events that impact us deeply. The holistic experience of this impact is what I consider trauma.

Trauma:

To me, trauma is an event or series of events on your spectrum of unfolding events that are so impactful emotionally, spiritually, and physically, it creates a void. Sometimes the trauma is so significant that our human expression cannot deal with it. Thus we fracture our lens. We should continue to make addressing trauma normal. Our mental health is critical to our survival during this human experience. When we do not address trauma, the void on the unfolding spectrum of events begins to impact your life in ways that may not have been intended. Imagine walking on a trail, and you trip and get back up. Tripping on this trail represents trauma or a void being created. Getting back up without checking to make sure that you did not hurt your-self represents suppressing what has happened to you even if you do not intend to do so. The further you walk down that trail without addressing the trauma, the void gets bigger and bigger making the journey more difficult. Sometimes trauma can cause us to be mentally held captive in that void on our spectrum, but we physically have moved forward because life does not stop. This misalignment can create an impact beyond what we realize. Unfortunately, we are left with a choice because some of the things we have defined to measure productivity—such as profit margins and time—do not always consider human experience. Get up and keep walking or get left behind. When the choice is made to get up and keep walking we eventually end up being swallowed by our void without realizing it. That void can show up in many different forms, such as anxiety, stress, depression, and more. Eventually, we create a sense of false reality that we operate within, looking through a fractured lens; this becomes our norm unless we choose to address it. I felt this when I experienced a family member dying by suicide for the first time; I was given three days for bereavement from my job without tapping into other resources such as Family Medical Leave or the grace of people with influence. Not knowing the importance of mental health, I went back to work in a daze, only to be negatively impacted by the general stress of work and life itself. I didn't know that I was sinking in a void that was crippling my ability to get through life.

Norms:

To me, norms are our consistent reality based on what we have experienced in our life. What I consider as normal may be different from what you consider normal. My norm was a tiny nuclear family in which I was the only child for an extended time. My grandparents spoiled me, my aunt and I were like Bonnie and Clyde, and my mom was an unstoppable force that made something out of nothing. Of course, I had other family members and friends. Still, the number of people I spent most of my life with within my younger years was minimal. This sharply contrasts with someone who is used to two parents in the family, brothers and sisters, cousins, all four grandparents, aunts, uncles, and more. I would be in total shock and probably sit in a corner somewhere if I was put in this situation because that is not my norm based on my life experiences. From this, we get a glimpse at the unseen spaces between me, who was raised with a small family, and someone who was raised with a bigger family. The way I approach things because of what was normal to me may differ from how they approach things. Guess what? That is okay! Our norms begin to shape how we interact within circumstances and with people. This becomes the lens that we look out of even when fractured.

Lens:

To me, your lens is how you view or process things and operate based on your norms. We should be mindful that it is possible to view things from your spectrum of events from a particular view. Remember, there is a possibility of you being misaligned mentally and physically; you always view things based on your lens. In other words, wherever you are mentally on your spectrum of life events combined with what is normal to you is the lens you view your present circumstances through. Your physical or survival lens is always there as it is required for you to make it through life. We aren't always aware of our spiritual lens unless taught or until an event causes us to see through that lens, or we are naturally programmed to see through that lens. Again, it can be difficult to shift between lenses, especially when something traumatic has happened on your spectrum of unfolding events. When we have a fractured physical lens, often due to a traumatic event or current circumstances, we cannot do things that align us with an outcome outside of a cycle or intentionally towards our purpose. Our lens, physical or spiritual, helps us to make decisions in our life.

Decisions:

To me, a decision is walking down a particular path when presented opportunities during an event on your spectrum of unfolding events; choice. For the sake of being consistent, there is no good, bad, or ugly decision; it's simply a decision. Beyond this decision are effects we are aware of and some that we are not. The impacts of our decision will always come back to us as this is the way life unfolds. The goal is to make decisions aligned with your purpose in life. This is not always easy especially given the lens you look through.

Life Experience:

To me, life experience is the totality of what you experience during your life up until the present moment. How far you look at the spectrum of unfolding events gives you context for why things are the way they are. An example of this is where you are right now in your life. Within the past 30 days, anything and everything that has happened helps you understand your life from a limited view. When you widen that view to maybe your entire life, it is possible to understand through your experience with life why you do what you do. We define the things we encounter in life as good, bad, and ugly. Still, I encourage you to not box your life experiences, regardless of how narrow or wide you may look at them. When we look at our life through a physical lens, we do not see the deeper meaning of circumstances and people. Remember that you are a small piece of source which simply is. It is necessary to strengthen your ability to shift to your spiritual lens to "SEE" the unseen spaces between us.

Formulas

- (Your Highest Sense of Self + Your Purpose) + Time and Chance (Circumstances and People + Decisions) = Your Birth

- Your Birth * (Family Trauma * Family Cycles) = Your Norms

- Your Norms + (Circumstances and People + Your Decisions) + (Your Trauma + Your Cycles) = Your Lens

- Your Birth * Your Norms * Your Lens (Circumstances and People + Your Decisions) = Life Experience

- Life Experience / (Circumstances + People) = Your Life Lessons

- Your Life Lessons + Application + Service to Others = Your Life Purpose

- Your Life Purpose + Collective Life Purpose of All Human Experiences = Source

Using myself as an example, I will help you understand what I have come to understand to be the process of life. Hopefully, this is another step towards helping you see the unseen spaces between us. I believe that source is, and that will always be, my answer regardless of what I decide to name it. I will never limit or constrict source as it is beyond my human comprehension, and I am okay with that. As those who came before me lived, there was a gap or an unfulfilled purpose in the world that needed to be birth.

Source allowed a fraction of its divine and unlimited being to step forth, which I now recognize was my highest sense of self. That unfilled purpose and I became one, and we needed divine timing to come forth in the world. Time and chance, the totality of life experiences from my entire family, and the individual decisions of my parents created a chance for them to meet. Before I was ever a thought in my parent's mind, I existed, just not in this physical form. Everything that my mother and father had gone through individually and collectively made it possible for me to be born June 8, 1989.

I was born into cycles and unspoken traumas of my families necessary to grow up the way I did; life was using this chaos to "aim me for my purpose." This perceived chaos created the life experiences that I would have. Eventually, on my spectrum of life events, trauma happened. As my spectrum of life events continued to unfold, my norms became my reality, and thus my lens was shaped. As far back as my family could be traced, everything that happened before I was born, although seen as chaotic, divinely and precisely crafted the chance for me to be here. The unaddressed traumas and cycles are burdens that I have to carry until I do things differently.

In addition to this, what makes it possible for purpose to not be fulfilled is that we all have free choice when presented with opportunities, the ability to make decisions during this human experience. My decisions within circumstances that involved people had hidden lessons meant to help me undo what has happened to my family and me, in addition to preparing me for my purpose if and only if I allowed it to be that way. Without shifting from a physical lens to a spiritual lens, I would simply be existing. Life constantly rearranges itself in a way that we are oriented towards our purpose in life. Although I know that I am naturally programmed to look through a spiritual lens, it took many traumatic events for my lens to get focused.

Trauma continued to pop up, creating voids that I did not address. Thus, my own cycle was created within the cycles of my family; eventually, I fractured my lens. Until a void was big enough for me to be forced to replace my fractured physical lens, causing me to actualize my spiritual lens, I was going through life trying to survive. Had I not made a choice to look through a different lens, my purpose may have never been fulfilled, as I may have arrived short of my destiny. This would cause a chain reaction in my family lines requiring someone else to step forth or someone else to be birth into this human experience with the charge of bringing that purpose forward. I recognize that I am simply a vessel being used to fulfill a needed purpose to help the world be better as others do the same thing. This is why it is essential not to have such a firm grip on things limited by this human experience. We are vessels being used to help the collective.

It was simply chaos—better known as divine timing—that allowed all of these things that we have defined to cross or mix in a way that made it possible for me to be here. You, my friend, are in the same ocean that I am, just in a different boat going to a different destination. The goal is to get everyone to align their boat with their destination to fulfill their purpose. Those who come behind us have less work and can focus on their purpose without struggling in survival mode. It is up to you to shift your lens and do things differently. You are breathing for a reason, purpose.

You are charged with something bigger than you realize, and it is needed to help the world be a better place. This is easier said than done because, again, we all have free choice, the ability to make decisions to walk down whatever path we choose. The majority of us are living and looking through a physical lens. This is neither good, bad, nor ugly; it just is. I choose to be intentional about the lens that I look out of given my purpose in life is to help people operate at their highest potential through self-awareness.

Observing this process of life helps me to understand and embrace the importance of helping people become aware of and strengthen their ability to shift to a spiritual lens. By sowing seeds in people through coaching, books, and speaking I can create a small pause in their cycle of survival mode; an opportunity for people to dig deep if only for a moment to start their own journey. The process of life is ongoing and will be ongoing until we all decide to look through our spiritual lens to see the unseen spaces between us.

Chapter of Forming My Lens

Quote:

"I can see a lot and still not understand until its meaning is revealed."

Analogy:

We were illiterate until we were taught what letters and numbers are and, more importantly, how to use them to derive meaning. Being taught, by self or others, is what forms your understanding to become literate. When the way you are taught is tainted, the way you derive meaning is also tainted. Unfortunately, you go through life at a disadvantage, not deriving true meaning from what you experience until you take action.

When I reflect on my spectrum of unfolding events, many things stick out to me. My family members are different; I mean that in the most loving way. The things they would say that I remember even as a 32-year-old make me smile like a little kid. There are certain sayings or phrases that I remember from some of them. For example, my mom would always tell me, "Loose lips sinks ships."

As a child, I literally imagined a ship sinking sometimes but eventually realized not to tell everything I knew. As an adult, I understand that I need to be mindful of what I say. This is probably why many people feel comfortable telling me things because I literally do not want to sink anyone's ship. If I am not mistaken, I am pretty sure I heard my grandmother say the same thing. Just like everyone else's grandmother, when people get to a certain age, they just don't care what comes out of their mouth. My grandmother spoiled me rotten. I got anything and everything I wanted between her and my grandfather.

Every once in a while, I would be doing too much and hear her say, "Sit your gnatty rump down!" It's almost like lightning and thunder went through the house. As a child, I may not have grasped what that meant, but I knew immediately to sit down before I got in trouble, no questions asked. Now I must admit, as an adult, I think where did these "old folk" get these sayings from, but nonetheless, I knew there was a deeper meaning behind it; you have to pause before you react to them. My grandmother was telling me, in only a way that she could, your actions and reactions will lead you to a consequence you do not want; stop and think about what you are doing. My grandmother was also a jokester.

We would laugh about the silliest things. Smiling without her dentures was one of them! If there was something to laugh about, even if she was the "butt of the joke," she would say it. My grandmother was a cancer survivor and wore wigs. She went back to school in her 50s to get her Bachelor's degree from South Carolina State University, and became a high school teacher, and boy, did she hit our family with a big joke one day! Now consider, my grandmother was a Black woman from the South raised during some callous times; she wasn't afraid of anything. One day we were sitting at the table, and my grandmother said a student asked if that wig was her own hair. Her response was, "Yeah, I bought it!" As a child, I was thinking, "Oh my gosh, did Granny just say that?"

To no one's surprise, all of the adults in my family were laughing and crying hysterically. I couldn't imagine a teacher saying that now. Even through the tears of laughing hysterically, there was a deeper meaning to this: mind your business. Speaking of business, as an only child, I was often an earshot away from adult conversations. Probably one of the things my grandmother said that I say myself is, "a hit dog will holler!" To this day, when there is an uncomfortable situation that I am observing, and someone starts to wiggle their way out of it, I hear my grandmother saying, "a hit dog will holler."

Of course, as a child, I literally imagined hearing a dog yelling out of pain, and I am thinking, why would someone hit a dog? That's mean! My grandmother was saying the truth was spoken, and it hit a nerve with someone. Man, do I miss my grandmother, no dentures and all! An aunt from my dad's side of the family and I are like two peas in a pod. She practically invented the common nap. Anytime I went to her, I knew a nap that would make you forget where you are and who you were was coming right after some freshly made lemon pepper wings! Of course, I love all of my aunts and uncles, but this was an "auntie." An "auntie" or "unc" is an aunt or uncle that you cling to in an extra-special way; source gave them some extra seasoning during the aunt or uncle recipe. But of course, this auntie would sprinkle some magic advice onto our peach pancakes.

The one piece of advice that she taught me, besides "back into parking spaces because you never know what will happen," was "people always respond based on their view of life." This didn't click immediately, I think I may have been waking up from a nap, but of course, as an adult, I get it. Anytime someone responds to a situation, gives you advice, or does something, it is based on everything in their life that has brought them to this point. Without even knowing it, as a young teen, I started to pause every time I felt someone said something that didn't sit right for an extra second to think, "That's how they view things." When I talk to my mom as an adult, she constantly reminds me, "There is a reason for your season."

As a self-aware adult, I immediately see that applies to circumstances and people. Even though it is not easy, I try to remember and apply that lesson during my ongoing spectrum of events. Even I am guilty of saying some things but maybe not as off the wall. Have you ever met someone who typically has the same response, but how they say that response tells you everything you need to know? Guilty, that's me! One of the things I catch myself saying a lot is, "Oh okay!"

Of course, that has many different meanings depending on the context. Still, for our sake, that is a friendly, short, and sweet way of saying, "I am listening to what you are saying, while processing and passing no judgement as you continue to tell me what is going on; life goes on." I am sure if I continue to think, I could come up with some pretty off-the-wall things my family has said, but these sayings will work just fine, helping you to see the unseen space between circumstances and people in your life.

I felt this book should be approached a little differently. A more applied approach will help you take a step back and start to "SEE" things differently. There are certain life events that I feel we all go through and could relate to. I would like to walk you through everyday life experiences to help you see things differently in hopes that you can do the same with circumstances and people in your life. I must admit that this level of knowing and understanding didn't happen overnight. It took a lot of work, but I assure you it was so worth it!

- Be mindful of what you say: "Loose lips sinks ships."

- Pause before you react: "Sit your gnatty rump down!"

- Mind your own business: "I paid for it."

- It's the truth, and it hit a nerve: "A hit dog will holler."

- It's the way they approach life: "People always respond based on their view of life."

- Impact beyond what you can see: "There is a reason for your season."

- Life goes on: "Oh okay."

Lessons from Self: Wake Up

In *A Gift of Peace and Purpose and Love and Meditation*, I detailed some traumatic life experiences. In talking with people, I feel that everyone goes through lessons that revolve around self. Next to my most important life lesson, love of self, was the lesson of self-awareness. Sometimes I feel as though there is a fog machine that someone turned on that puts everyone in a zombie-like daze; everyone is just trying to survive. This fog machine keeps us at lower-level thinking, and eventually, we look up at the end of our life. We do not remember anything besides the 30 to 40 years we spent at a job and the missed moments of family, friends, and what ifs that we will never get back.

The fog can really be anything like excessive use of your phone, excessive working, excessive use of social and news media, obsession with what makes people unique and different, deep attachment to worldly stuff, and anything that distracts you from operating at your highest potential while in the present moment. I try my best not to watch tv as much but try to be in nature a lot, look in people's eyes while talking when it doesn't violate their cultural norms, and do anything I can to ground myself in the present moment to stay away from the fog. Of all things, I feel technology, specifically the excessive use of social media, is a prime example of this fog that keeps us at lower-level thinking. Technology seems to be restricting some of our thinking skills. For example, I cannot remember a phone number because of technology besides my mom's phone number, 911, and the numbers I use consistently for work. Social media has a heavy influence on behavior.

If I take a step back, I feel excessive use of social media is done by people who may be looking for a means to not deal with their trauma, quick to point out, comment, or laugh at something someone else is going through to keep what they go through hidden or suppressed. This fog or this way of life is slowly but surely making it easier for people not to think and it's killing them silently. Cancel culture can be dangerous when the circumstance that we look at is too narrow a view on the individual; look at the full picture, especially intent. If I could be frank, it seems like a game of systems versus humanity versus nature; the systems are winning. Systems are harmless through a physical lens but through a spiritual lens, you see how people's true potential are locked or limited keeping them at lower-level thinking. This could be how the education system is set up, corporate America being focused on profit and not employees' well-being, government housing, social media, the medical insurance industry, and even the American dream.

I personally feel, to some extent, the way life has been set up for minorities is intended to keep us from achieving the American dream and keep us as a means to fulfill the American dream for others. Suppose I am put through a system that keeps me thinking at lower levels. In that case, I can only do things differently when I step out of the system through higher-level thinking. Humanity is simply people trying to survive and do the right thing. I always wonder when do people have the time to heal themselves? Just as I stated earlier when I experience trauma, we have to contribute to society, be a parent, partner, student, and everything else that takes away from us. Not saying that these are bad things, but when we have traumatic events, there is no "adult corner" that everyone is running to have time to address what has happened we have to survive. Pause for a moment to ask yourself, have I truly healed the root cause of each and every trauma in my life? Nature is simply the natural and raw unfolding of life only influenced by the decisions that we make with lower or higher-level thinking.

This ongoing battle between these three things is the right formula for mental health issues, especially when trauma is added to the equation. Suppose a child grows up in an underdeveloped area. Systems such as their underfunded education system, broken public transit, unsafe housing, poor food options and more limit them to potential outputs of these systems working together. As a result of these systems, the child grows up exposed to only what the system allows them to be exposed to and thus their thinking is limited. Nature will continue to unfold, putting the child in circumstances with people in which they can only use their limited thinking; their possibility of becoming a statistic is infinitely more than someone who contrast this experience.

Suppose a child grows up in an area that has access to a lot of resources. Everything that this child has access to helps develop their way of thinking which ideally would be better than the child in the underdeveloped area. The quality of life is substantially better even if they do not reach a certain level of awareness. What these two children have in common is that they are both human and nature does not care who they are or what their background is. A sincere question could be asked to understand why it is so political to ensure people have resources that equal the playing field.

My simple answer as I've spoken about before is: profit. Who will execute on the vision of the child who had access to a lot of resources? The child who grew up in an underdeveloped area limited to their lower-level thinking. This child grows up to be a person trying to survive who does not have time to pick apart the systems that had a heavy influence on their life. They only have time or the capacity to vote on the promise of someone who aims to positively change their life limited by a system that is eating itself.

We wonder why famine, war, and other horrible events continue to happen. Without the space to heal, the masses cannot focus on these things, leaving it up to those who have influence and somewhat broken free of the system to insert positive change. The individual purpose(s) bestowed within us, collectively can help with world issues if only people have the awareness to see it and act upon it. I hope it is easy to see how and why mental health is so important as traumatic events only compound the effects of what we go through. It's never easy to break free of the ongoing battle of systems versus humanity versus nature but I aim to make it possible for those who are open to it.

My lesson of wake up or self-awareness was triggered through traumatic events, as I alluded to earlier. Each opportunity I had to learn self-awareness through circumstances and people was overlooked because I was in a fog, trying to survive. Systems had filtered me to only focus on achievement and what's next, as a human I simply wanted to survive only thinking of achievement and what's next as a qualifier to being accepted and belonging, and nature continued to unfold. The constant stress of worrying about what's next or how to make more money, instead of my inner expression made it possible for life to bring lessons through circumstances and people in a way only it could. The thing that I realized about circumstances that I found myself in was that it required me to reflect on my decisions.

After a decision was made, I realized after dealing with the consequences that there was something that I could have done differently or a path that I could have walked down that may have been less tumultuous. The people that were in these circumstances were taking advantage of me. They may not have known that they were carrying a lesson with them, but they certainly knew what they were doing. What was intended to be a lesson of think through your decisions from a place of clarity turned into a cycle that mentally kept me in the past with these traumatic events as life moved forward. In this part of my life, what I wanted was someone to love me or accept me.

Through my physical lens, what I saw was broken promises and abuse. In the unseen spaces between the circumstance, these people and I, my spiritual lens allowed me to "SEE" that they were a hurt person hurting me and that all my answers were within me. When I created the space to take a step back and think, I could look through their lens to understand why they did what they were doing; they were the product of an ongoing battle and trauma. It helped me realize that the circumstance was more than someone who could not keep their promises or someone who didn't know anything other than what they saw or were taught. I identified the underlying lesson of "wake up" to better manage myself and be more intentional about my actions through self-awareness.

I could easily hear my grandmother saying, "a hit dog will holler," in some of the instances when I confronted someone about something that was done with ill intent. There was an uncomfortable feeling of backpedaling or changing what they said to fit what was now the clear truth. Even when situations were trying to be flipped to be my fault, I had to realize "people always respond based on their view of life" because doing this was normal to them and what had gotten them this far in life. When reflecting on these situations, I had to ask myself many questions that helped me get to the root of my not being self-aware. We should quickly learn the lesson intended for us to "wake up" and step out of the fog of survival mode because the lessons of self can never be learned without doing so. It requires that we dig deeper and look at the spectrum of unfolding life events from a view that captures everything that caused us to form the lens we now look through. When that lens needs attention, take the best steps to address your lens so that you can "SEE" what is not blatantly apparent through the physical lens that we look through.

Reflection:

Now that we have talked about the lesson of self, let's pause and reflect on the answers to these questions:

- Is there a set of circumstances or people in my life that causes me to reflect on the decisions that I have made?

- If multiple circumstances and people, what do they have in common?

- What could be the underlying lesson that, when applied, prevents me from being in the same circumstances or dealing with the same people?

- What would happen if I missed the lesson?

- Why do I think these circumstances or specific people are necessary for me?

- What could I be intended to teach by being a part of this circumstance or person's life?

- Now that I see the unseen space between myself, the circumstance, and the person(s), what do I need to keep, stop, and start doing?

Application:

After reflecting on your answers to the above questions, consistently apply lessons learned that you have identified. At the end of each day, journal by capturing each moment that you applied your lessons learned, what you got done, what you want to finish the next day, thoughts that consistently pop up, people who you interacted with, and all your emotions. Continue to ask yourself these questions:

- What am I asking for intentionally and unintentionally through my thoughts, words, and deeds?

- What is my current circumstance(s) that bring discomfort?
- Who are the people in my life?
- What was the outcome of me applying my lessons learned?

Lessons from Relationships: Be Intentional and Use Your Voice

Relationships are so much work! Not just romantic relationships but relationships in all forms. I am growing to accept that sometimes relationships reflect what we need in that present moment and what we need to heal within ourselves. I do not think we take a moment to realize that other people are doing the same just as we live our lives. Just as we have things that we need to heal, others have to do the same thing. What we must be aware of is how we govern ourselves within these relationships.

After all, we cannot control what anyone else does or thinks, which is why self-awareness is vital. This helps us to realize "there is a reason for your season." Remember that time and chance provide opportunities for lives to cross paths. You may even notice this amongst your family, friends, and other people in your life. When you finally have the chance to talk to someone about the previous brief interactions that you had with each other, you may realize that there was a reason that the chance for you to cross paths at that particular time may not have been right based on what you needed.

Essentially, the snapshot of your life that you view has a reason for specific circumstances and people. Sometimes these relationships are meant to be close, and sometimes they are not meant to be. I identified the underlying lesson of "be intentional" and "use your voice" to better navigate various relationships, including the one with myself. In this case, there were very rocky relationships that caused me discomfort. It was almost as if that circumstance was not intended to last long, so there was no reason for me to get comfortable or close to that person.

These relationships were triggering me so that how I did things before would not help me receive the positive intent the relationship was supposed to provide. I had to do something different for the lesson to be identified, learned and applied to get a different outcome than before. Unless I needed to interact with people in these rocky relationships, I could see my grandmother at the kitchen table saying, "I paid for it." I minded my business. In other words, I knew that there was a reason behind these rocky relationships. Still, I did not create the space for us to intertwine more than I felt was necessary and thus the majority of my responses were "Oh okay." I needed to ensure there was enough space between myself and the other person to dig deeper to understand why I was responding the way I was; what was the trigger that caused me to feel unsettled. I used my self-awareness as a tool to act with intention and strategically use my voice.

What I wanted in this phase of my life was peaceful interactions with people to get through life. Through my physical lens, I saw people who were just mean and honestly didn't care what people thought about them. In the unseen spaces between the circumstance, these people and I, my spiritual lens allowed me to "SEE" an opportunity for me to change how I approached life, more specifically people, by being intentional with my actions and using my voice in a way that helped them on their path. Looking through their lens, I saw their inability to manage close relationships or protect themselves based on their past trauma. These relationships that we find ourselves in are ways to make it through life while learning necessary life lessons. Without these relationships, there would not be an opportunity to learn lessons intended to prepare you for your purpose.

Reflection:

Now that we have talked about the lesson of relationships, let's pause and reflect on the answers to these questions:

- Is there a person in my life that causes me to be uncomfortable or challenges me? Why?

- Is there a person in my life that I am drawn to positively because I want them to grow or see something in them? Why?

- In either situation, what are the common characteristics of your interactions?

- What could be the underlying lesson or message intended to be given or received?

- What would happen if this person or I missed the lesson?

- Why do I think these circumstances or specific person(s) are necessary?

- Now that I see the unseen space between myself, the circumstance, and the person(s), what do I need to keep, stop, and start doing?

Application:

After reflecting on your answers to the above questions, consistently apply lessons learned that you have identified. At the end of each day, journal by capturing each moment that you applied your lessons learned, what you got done, what you want to finish the next day, thoughts that consistently pop up, people who you interacted with, and all your emotions. Continue to ask yourself these questions:

- What am I asking for intentionally and unintentionally through my thoughts, words, and deeds?

- What is my current circumstance(s) that bring discomfort?

- Who are the people in my life?

- What was the outcome of me applying my lessons learned?

Lessons from Work: Be Optimistic

Who invented work? Why? Who wants to get up early in the morning to do something that they do not enjoy doing? On top of that, to be expected to do it consistently at a high-performance level in a horrible environment, which is a proven formula for anxiety, stress, and burnout? The one thing that most of us have in common about work is that we have to do it to survive.

It wasn't until I consistently looked through my spiritual lens that I realized work can be enjoyable if you realize how the circumstance and people you find yourself with aligning with a more significant meaning beyond what you see now. This takes practice, of course, but once you get comfortable looking through the right lens to dig deeper, the positive intent will become more and more prominent. What I hated about work initially was that it added no value to my life besides paying an endless supply of bills. Utility, gas, car, medical bills; I still don't understand why healthcare isn't free; I imagine someone isn't ready to pull the plug on that cash cow. For most people, I feel what makes work survivable is the people you interact with regularly.

I could go on and on about the importance of culture and effective leadership, but your current line of work is more important to your purpose than someone's bottom line. When I became very clear about my goals in life and started to take a step back to see the deeper meaning of things, I realized even the jobs that I wasn't too fond of were somehow still tied to my purpose. Even if it wasn't blatantly obvious, eventually, skills learned from that role were easily applicable to my purpose. At the end of 2020, when I decided to take a job that wasn't something that would make me truly happy, I was content knowing that there was still something applicable to my purpose. I identified the underlying lesson of "be optimistic" to grow my motivation from knowing that the skills learned in that job helped me in a way that would make my purpose more obtainable. I used self-awareness to be intentional about my actions and the way I used my voice. In this part of my life, I wanted to have a peaceful job to pay my bills and survive.

Through a physical lens, I saw just that, a means to pay bills and survive. In the unseen spaces between the circumstance, these people, and I, my spiritual lens allowed me to "SEE" I was indirectly preparing for my purpose in life, waiting for the opportunity to leap given the right time and chance. I saw myself as strategic, dependable, a high performer, and relatable through other people's lenses. Being uncomfortable in this job was the necessary soil for me to grow. It just took self-awareness for me to realize this and continue to move forward.

Sometimes we see optimism in other people, which motivates us to become more optimistic. We have no idea what people have gone through most of the time, but to be optimistic, despite life unfolding with unpleasant circumstances, takes a lot of courage. Even when people choose not to be optimistic, I remind myself, "people always respond based on their view of life."

Reflection:

Now that we have talked about the lessons of work, let's pause and reflect on the answers to these questions:

- Considering there are millions of jobs available, why am I currently working where I am?

- What opportunity does this job provide circumstances and people to come into my life and help me towards my purpose?

- Am I in a position where I can help people in pursuit of their purpose?

- What could be the underlying reason I am at this job as a part of the circumstances in my life that may involve people?

- What would happen if I missed the reason?

- Why do I think these circumstances or specific person(s) are necessary?

- Now that I see the unseen space between myself, the circumstance, and the person(s), what do I need to keep, stop, and start doing?

Application:

After reflecting on your answers to the above questions, consistently apply lessons learned that you have identified. At the end of each day, journal by capturing each moment that you applied your lessons learned, what you got done, what you want to finish the next day, thoughts that consistently pop up, people who you interacted with, and all your emotions. Continue to ask yourself these questions:

- What am I asking for intentionally and unintentionally through my thoughts, words, and deeds?
- What is my current circumstance(s) that bring discomfort?
- Who are the people in my life?
- What was the outcome of me applying my lessons learned?

Lessons from Life: Love Yourself, Be Present, Be Patient, and Be Resilient

What is the meaning of life? Why are we here? What is the intended purpose behind all of us living at the exact same time on the same rock? I personally feel we should individually answer those questions. Still, I do know for sure that we suggest the meaning of life through our actions. If you were like me, my actions were going to work, eating, paying bills, sleeping, and if I had enough money, some fun here and there. There is nothing wrong with that, but I choose differently for myself and the generations behind me.

My consistent actions gave no outcome that motivated me to step out of the fog of trying to survive. Thus my life was meaningless but valued by others at whatever I was being paid at the time. Until we start to "SEE" the unseen spaces between us, until we apply lessons learned, until we find the crux of our lessons learned and circumstances we have found ourselves in, until we leverage our gifts and talents, and until we are of service to people with positive intent life is meaningless. Until we associate our actions with a reason, life is meaningless. I identified the underlying lesson of "love yourself, be present, be patient, and be resilient" to equip myself to get through life in a fulfilling way. You must love yourself to ensure that you take care of yourself first and then others.

When you do not take care of yourself, your body will tell you and eventually force you. Life is so short, and we have to experience this beautiful place we call earth which requires us to be present in every moment. Hone in on your senses to ensure where you are mentally and physically are aligned. Allow nature to be the gym you need to physically, spiritually, and emotionally be fit. Even when you have to step into survival mode temporarily, know that it is a part of a process and remain patient with yourself. Things that are worth having are never received overnight or quickly.

Can you imagine the satisfaction of honoring your purpose through honest hard work and being rewarded with fulfillment and joy? There is no amount of money or worldly things that can replace that. Even if you want to enjoy the luxuries of life, which there is nothing wrong with, at a minimum, learn the importance of self-awareness, intention, using your voice, and being optimistic. I always hear people suggest what they could have, would have, or should have done to compare them to now. Everything happens for a reason which is within the unseen spaces between circumstances, people, and you.

Life is always going to continue. I won't say that everyone can't start looking for the deeper meaning of life events, but it will take effort from everyone who is and will be on that journey. It takes self-awareness, being intentional, using your voice, optimism, and a host of other things while helping others along the way. I can guarantee it may not be easy, especially when you have to sit in traffic to go to work, go through the TSA line at the airport, work with people who you don't care for, and be family members with people who don't act like they were raised under the same roof. I try to give people and myself as much grace as possible. We are human! That's why I say "oh okay" a lot to let things roll off my back.

There is no need to get all stressed out about something that has happened or is out of your control. Even though it would be impossible to be relaxed in every situation, creating that habit of letting things roll off your back delays anxiety and stress enough for you to think through situations that happen. This may be why I don't talk that much unless spoken to. Engaging with people is vital but don't allow for "loose lips to sink ships." Everything doesn't need to be said as people may not handle or properly receive what you have to say.

I personally find out more by listening than speaking. Now, I must be clear if I haven't before; this is not an easy path to walk down. There are plenty of times when I go about everyday life, and I interact with someone that makes me forget all of my meditation practices. Catching myself by hearing my grandmother say, "sit your gnatty rump down," has saved me many consequences and embarrassment. This has literally been a multi-year journey for me. Even now, sometimes it's hard to be motivated and optimistic. There are days when I cannot keep focused on the end goal and get discouraged.

Even now, as I try to get into human resources at work, I have heard no more than I can count; that's discouraging. I know that I have to make a living for myself until I can solely focus on my purpose. It's difficult to remain optimistic but self-awareness gives me the space to "SEE" that there is a reason time and chance are not aligning. Knowing this I must be intentional with my actions, use my voice strategically, and remain optimistic. Why focus on attaining something with impact confined within a company when purpose can shift the world. For this revelation, I am grateful.

I just refuse to stay in any circumstance that doesn't pull me closer to my purpose of helping people operate at their highest potential through self-awareness. Even considering all of the things that I have been through, I know that it could have been a lot worse if I didn't wake up when I did. What I wanted in life was to survive as I was simply just existing. Through my physical eyes, I saw life quickly passing me by while being my biggest critic and hurdle. I was trying to do more with fewer resources as quickly as possible without showing people that I was weak. In the unseen spaces between the circumstance, these people, and I, my spiritual lens allowed me to "SEE" the importance of loving yourself, being in the present moment, patient, and never giving up.

Reflection:

Now that we have talked about life, let's pause and reflect on the answers to these questions:

- Does my lens need attention?
- What are things I now realize?
- Why do I think these circumstances or specific person(s) are necessary based on what I have been through?
- What do these lessons, circumstances, and people have in common?
- How can I be of service to people with my lessons learned, gifts and talents?
- What would happen if I did not serve people with my purpose in life?

- Now that I see the unseen space between myself, the circumstance, and the person(s), what do I need to keep, stop, and start doing?

Application:

After reflecting on your answers to the above questions, consistently apply lessons learned that you have identified. At the end of each day, journal by capturing each moment that you applied your lessons learned, what you got done, what you want to finish the next day, thoughts that consistently pop up, people who you interacted with, and all your emotions. Continue to ask yourself these questions:

- What am I asking for intentionally and unintentionally through my thoughts, words, and deeds?
- What is my current circumstance(s) that bring discomfort?
- Who are the people in my life?
- What was the outcome of me applying my lessons learned?

Dear Future Generation

Lead with your highest sense of self by looking through your spiritual lens. This will never put you in a position to be hurt but allow you to identify, learn, and apply life lessons more easily. Circumstances and people are used to bring these lessons to you as you go throughout this human experience. Lessons are necessary for you to be the best version of yourself so that you can honor your purpose in life. You must use self-awareness to navigate through life so that you can honor your purpose.

It's almost as if you are born into the world playing double-dutch. The people on each end of the rope represents systems as there are more than you, you represent humanity jumping in the middle, and the ropes being spun is nature in its constant unfolding. Each rope represents circumstances and people meant to teach you lessons. For you to jump from between the ropes you must identify, learn, and apply the lesson. Look through your spiritual lens, "SEE" everything around you to make intentional choices that will help you jump at the right time; self-awareness is the key.

I learned of a Japanese term called Ikigai, which I understand to mean "A reason for being." It simply suggests your purpose lies at the heart of four principles: do something that you love, that the world needs, that you are great at, and can be paid for. With good intentions and aligning your actions towards your purpose, this concept is very genuine. Explore the world and try different things that do not intend to harm you or put you in danger. Protect what is most sacred to you but do not allow deep attachment to keep you from being open to new things.

In this limited life, we can never comprehend all things. What has been passed to you is only a fraction of what the world has to offer. The summation of what I do in my life can be viewed as the ceiling upon which you stand on as a foundation for your life. Know that your purpose is the sun and you are the planets around it; embrace that you are the planet and use the power of your Sun to make life easier for those that need you. Everything that you need is within, release to receive while trusting the process and its unfolding; everything will be alright.

Conclusion

Without even realizing it, a physical lens could easily allow you to see another one of the seven billion people on earth who just happened to be where you are. A spiritual lens would allow you to see that there is something that you are learning or teaching through your circumstances with people; this is required for your purpose to be handled well. There is a reason that I am typing this book. There is a reason why it is easy for me to listen to others and hear what they say and do not say. There is a reason that the questions that I come up with can catch people off guard and make them think deeply.

There is a reason that I am so easy to get along with and to trust. There is a reason that I push people, including myself, to be the best that they can be regardless of their current circumstances. The circumstances and people, trauma, decisions, lessons, and revelations intertwine and point to my purpose in life. As stated before, my purpose in life is to help people operate at their highest sense of self through self-awareness. The ability to shift lenses makes it blatantly obvious why I went through everything that I went through and why I am made in a unique way that I am made.

This goes for you as well, but a purpose only you can fulfill. Everyone chasing after their purpose could stop a lot of what we perceive as bad things from happening. Your purpose has a chance to come forward regardless of where you are in this short glimpse of life. Your purpose, your gifts, and your talents are not meant for you but for the world to be better off than it was when you got here. We need more people chasing their purpose, and the world would be a better place. Embrace the process of becoming what you will always be, just with the ability to shift from a physical lens to a spiritual lens. Continue to look for the unseen spaces between us. Your life will never be the same.